HUMAN NATURE

An Essay

By

WILLIAM LYON PHELPS

First published in 1931

British Library Cataloguing-in-Publication Data
A catalogue record for this book is available
from the British Library

CONTENTS

WILLIAM LYON PHELPS 5

HUMAN NATURE.................................7

WILLIAM LYON PHELPS

William Lyon Phelps was born on 2nd January 1865, in New Haven, Conneticut, United States.

Phelps earned a B.A. in 1887, writing his thesis on the Idealism of George Berkeley. He then gained an M.A. in 1891 from Yale and his PhD from Harvard in the same year.

During his time a Yale, he offered a course in modern novels which brought the university considerable attention both nationally and internationally. This was quite controversial at the time and Phelps was pressured to give up the course, but eventually, due to popular demand, reinstated it outside the official curriculum.

In 1892, Phelps married Annabel Hubbard, sister of childhood friend Frank Hubbard, and the couple moved to the family estate overlooking Lake Huron. Phelps christened it "The House of the Seven Gables", after the Nathanial Hawthorne story of the same name.

He became a very popular figure at Yale but also as an inspirational orator. He went on lecture tours that drew large audiences, speaking on the virtues of modern literature. He also preached regularly at the Huron City Methodist Episcopal Church and attracted such large crowds that the church was remodelled twice in five years to accommodate them.

Phelps published many essays on modern and European literature, including titles such as *Essays on Modern Novelists* (1910), *Some Makers of American Literature* (1923), and *As I Like it* (1923).

After his retirement from Yale in 1933, after 41 years of service, Phelps continued his public speaking, preaching, and writing a newspaper column. He also sat on book selection committees and acted as a judge for the Pulitzer Prize for literature.

His wife, Annabel, died from a stroke in 1939 and Phelps died four years later, in 1943.

HUMAN NATURE

WHEN I WAS EIGHT years old and was spending a week-end visiting my Aunt Libby Linsley, at her home in Stratford on the Housatonic, a middle-aged man called one evening, and after a polite skirmish with my aunt, he devoted his attention to me. At that time I happened to be excited about boats, and the visitor discussed the subject in a way that seemed to me particularly interesting. After he left, I spoke of him with enthusiasm. What a man! And how tremendously interested in boats! My aunt informed me he was a New York lawyer; that he cared nothing whatever about boatstook not the slightest interest in the subject. "But why then did he talk all the time about boats?" "Because he is a gentleman. He saw you were interested in boats, and he talked about the things he knew would interest and please you. He made himself agreeable." I never forgot my aunt's remark.

Like many boys of my time, I learned about religion and morality from my mother, and about etiquette, clothes, and the ways of the world from my aunt. For some reason virgin aunts were always more worldly minded than mothers.

On this occasion Aunt Libby made clear the difference between a gentleman and a bore. A gentleman puts his companions or guests or casual acquaintances at their ease; he is considerate; he has tact; he draws out the contents of the other man's mind, and thus enables him to appear at his best. A bore talks only about the things that interest him himself; he has little perception of the impression he is making, or of the actual state of mind of his victim.

Perhaps the final test of a gentleman is his attitude toward children. I wonder if all men remember as vividly as I do the occasions when grownup people treated us neither with contempt nor with indifference nor with what is worse, grinning condescension-I' And how is my little man today?"-but with unassumed respect. The few occasions in my childhood when strangers treated me with courtesy produced an indelible impression.

In conversation, the time and the place and the subject should harmonise. There are talkers who have a positive genius for the inopportune.

Not so many years ago, as I was leaving my house to walk to the Yale-Harvard football game, I met a man I knew only slightly, who insisted on discussing literature all the way to the arena of combat. There were the streets crowded with an excited throng, all-except my friend thinking of only one thing; in the midst of this joyous, laughing, noisy multitude, this man wished to know what I thought of the contemporary condition of American poetry.

The relative importance of poetry and football had nothing to do with the occasion. As humour is out of place at a funeral, so a discussion of literature is out of place at the great game of the year. A man's soul is of more importance than a trivial engagement; but if a zealous evangelist stops a man running to catch a train to enquire about his salvation, it is probable he will miss both.

A famous German philosopher, Lotze, who had more influence on the life and character of the late Lord Haldane than any other teacher, defined existence as follows: *To be is to be in relations.* That is to say, a living thing is living because it is in relations, in connexion with something. A dead body is dead because it has ceased to hold any relation to any other thing in the universe. Hence, the more interests a man has the more he is alive. It is unfortunate for boys and girls in school and college if their friends are confined to persons of similar taste, "who talk the same language." Such restriction is still more unfortunate for men and women in society. Every one ought to be on intimate terms with every kind of human being. Theodore Roosevelt was a scholar and a statesman; he had friends in all groups and classes, from missionaries to crooks. Gene Tunney was heavyweight champion boxer of the world; in addition to his friends in sporting circles, he numbers among his intimate associates clergymen, head masters of schools, leaders in business; and also the most famous man of letters and the most famous man of music in the world-Bernard Shaw and Richard Strauss.

Affectation and pretence are almost invariably the sign of a small mind, of a personage who is distinctly minor. Men who have reached the summit of their profession are almost invariably without pose-they are natural and unaffected. They do not smell of their job, and have none of the traditional trappings of the part. When Lockhart first met Robert Browning, he exclaimed, "Why, he isn't in the least like a damned literary man." But when you see a fifth rate minor poet, he is likely to advertise in his hair and in his clothes and in his speech that he is not like ordinary persons-he is forsooth a Bard.

Many actors play a part more earnestly off the stage than on. A conceited actor was once looking with a friend at a portrait of David Garrick, and he remarked: "They say I look more and more like Garrick every day." "Yes," was the answer, "and less and less like him every night." We so readily expect actors on the stage to act like actors instead of like men, that when a truly great actor or actress appears on the boards we are thrilled by *naturalness,* by the absence of conventional mannerisms.

Affectation is founded on fear. It is a species of bluff. The person fears he will be found out. "A little learning is a dangerous thing," said Pope. It makes one too careful. So the social climber has the veneer of good manners, and "watches out" continually, whereas the born aristocrat does not care what anyone thinks. One with a little learning cannot afford to make a mistake and therefore makes many. The true scholar is the first to admit that there is no such thing as human infallibility.

The great poets, novelists, dramatists have as a rule simple and natural manners. Many years ago I spent an evening at his house in Paris with Maurice Maeterlinck. He had published a number of plays that dealt with the uncanny and the supernatural, and I dare say many imagined him to be a pale, dreamy, lackadaisical person. On the contrary, he was absolutely common-sensible, frank, hearty, downright-the best word to describe him would be the word jovial. He offered me a cigarette, and being somewhat rattled, I stuck the lighted end in my mouth, which gave him much innocent mirth.

Bernard Shaw, who with his pen has slain tens of thousands, gives one in conversation the impression of cheerful kindliness. His manner is as free from cynicism as it is from conceit. One feels he would be the best of friends in or out of need. I suppose there is nothing so tiresome to the true hero as hero-worship. Lindbergh literally takes the wings of the morning to escape from it. A hundred years ago a stranger met the Duke of Wellington on the street, and asked if he might shake hands. He then remarked, "Now I will tell my grandchildren this is the hand that shook the hand of the conqueror at Waterloo." The Iron Duke replied, "Oh, don't make a damn fool out of yourself."

There is no doubt the most conceited people in the world are the most obscure-I don't put it the other way around; I don't say the most obscure are the most conceited, for there are plenty of obscure persons who are the salt of the earth. The most erudite scholar measures himself by the highest standards and feels ignorant-the greatest writer, I suppose, knows how far short he is of the ideal, and hence is modest; but the man of small ability and large ambition has no sure basis of comparison and overestimates his production. A man who has never succeeded in getting a single line into print often thinks his verse is as good as Milton's} his plays as good as Shakespeare's, his novels equal to Tolstoi's.

Many manuscripts sent in good faith to every magazine would astound the readers if they were printed.

In the last analysis, human nature is an inexplicable mystery;

it is, as the Russians say, a dark forest. Browning spent his whole life as a specialist in human nature, and he was forced to admit that he knew nothing about it. All he could do was to record instances of "queer" behaviour, but he ridiculed those who were cocksure of others' motives, while the great physicians were so often mistaken about bodily symptoms.

"You are sick, that's sure"-they say; "Sick of what?" they disagree. "'Tis the brain"-thinks Doctor A; "'Tis the heart"-holds Doctor B; "The liver-my life I'd lay!"

"The lungs!" "The lights!"

Ah me!

So ignorant of man's whole Of bodily organs plain to see So sage and certain, frank and free, About what's under lock and keyMan's soul!

Those whom we think we know best will often surprise us by not running true to form; no wonder, then, we are often amazed by finding in

strangers some trait absolutely contrary to their facial expression. Eugene O'Neill, in his play *The Great God Brown*, built a powerful drama on the idea that everyone wears a mask. When I was six years old, I learned for the first time the difference between a mask and reality. I was walking up Chapel Street, New Haven, and as I neared the corner of College Street, I saw a very old man, bent over with infirmities, wearing a copious white beard. He kept stopping pedestrians and asked in a broken, pathetic whine, "Won't you give a poor old man a penny?" I looked at him with childish pity. Suddenly he came over to me and whispered "Don't you worry about me! I've got loads of money." He whipped out of his pocket a canvas bag, containing a pint of solid cash. Then he lifted his beard, and behold, he was a smoothshaven young man. He laughed gaily. The next instant he had turned, stopped a passer, and repeated his begging question with tears in his voice. Now why do you suppose he made that revelation to a little boy? Did some impulse force him? Was the expression on my face so sincere that he could not bear to deceive a child, or was it that he could not endure to have me go away sorrowful for one who was so well able to take care of himself? I did not give him away.

Some thirty years later, I stood in line at a railway-ticket-office, and marvelled at the courtesy and deference shown by the ticket-seller to the silly and flustered purchasers. Their questions, it seemed to me, would have ruffled the patience of job. "How much did you say it was? Are you sure the train stops there? Is there no train before the next one?" To all these superfluous enquiries the ticket seller replied with sweet and smiling courtesy, showing no trace of irritation or impatience. When I finally reached him, I quietly complimented him on his steady politeness. He broke out in a stream of profanity. I must have touched a nerve and released a pent-up spring in this apparently patient man.

One reason I have never been able to take a cynical or depreciatory view of the mass of mankind is because I know so many specimens of so many different classes. I do not admire that oft-quoted saying by Carlyle to the effect that the population of the earth is mostly fools. In the first place, I cannot make myself feel that tremendous sense of personal superiority to the average run of mankind which is necessary to complacent cynicism; in the second place, while the history of mankind in general is "whole centuries of folly, noise, and sin," men, women, and children in particular often show noble traits and characteristics.

There are many snobs and selfsatisfied individuals who the moment they enter a crowded trolley car or subway, glare at the other passengers in the firm belief that every one except the glarer is a fool or a knave.

I claim no credit either for human sympathy or for loving-kindness or for democratic sentiment when I say that I could not feel that way if I tried. For I am certain that every person in that crowd has some fine quality; is perhaps at this very moment under appalling difficulties displaying a courage far greater than mine would or could be.

Just as the level of intelligence and morality in a mob may be lower than the lowest member of it-for the rotten apple in the barrel not only degrades the others but steadily itself grows more rotten-so a consideration of humanity in the mass is neither edifying nor cheering; hence it will usually be found that the cynics and the scorners and the haters are *lookers* on. That is, they are as they are because they are ignorant.

If they knew more individuals from all classes and knew them intimately, their affection and respect for men and women would rise. How often we read in the newspapers or take an oral report of what some man is supposed to have said, and we immediately decide that the man is a fool. Then perhaps later we meet and talk with this very same person, and find he is anything but a foolhe is a man of sense and good judgment. All we needed for the correct understanding of him was a little more knowledge.

In international affairs, it is probable that a complete knowledge by the citizens of one country of the citizens of another country, would make war impossible. In 194, the average Englishman supposed that the average German lieutenant was inhuman, some kind of monster; the soldiers who fought against him knew better. The average German thought Sir Edward Grey-a quiet English gentleman who loved birds-was a dark, designing, smooth, hypocritical villain, plotting with lies and treachery against the peace of Europe. Lichnowsky knew better.

Mr. Gerald Stanley Lee was on the right track when he suggested that millions and millions of dollars be expended by each country to *advertise* its real nature and aims in other countries. Spend at least part of the money now devoted to threats-for every battleship is a threat-on disseminating knowledge. It was a happy idea of the Australians last year to send several hundred Australian boys around the world and have them entertained by the citizens of every town they visited in their separate homes. Why not send the entire House of Commons on a similar journey? It pays to advertise.

The road to sympathy with and affection for human beings lies through knowledge and more knowledge. The British reviewers who ridiculed the poetry of Keats called him Johnny Keats. His brother said "John is no more like Johnny Keats than he is like the Holy Ghost." Our conceptions of other persons are frequently, perhaps commonly, as far from the truth as that. I have just been reading a book of intimate recollections of Gladstone, written by his son, called *After Thirty* Years. He wrote it because every recent biography of his father seemed to the family, who had the best knowledge of him, to present a portrait grotesquely unlike the original.

Now I suppose no biographer except Boswell and the Old Testament writers has succeeded in telling the truth about his hero. Hence Lord Gladstone, instead of writing a biography, put down a succession of anecdotes and instances which show that Gladstone was not in the least like the man set forth in all seriousness by the professional portrait painters.

As we grow older, we are less and less likely to call others insane. Many prominent men have had the weakness to imagine that every one who differs from them is both intellectually inferior and morally delinquent; and there are persons who secretly think that those who hold contrary opinions are at least partially crazy. Tolerance comes with years and experience, because years and experience bring knowledge. Just as two persons talking in Russian seem funny to an American boy, when they are really not funny at all; so there are persons who seem to others insane, simply because the others lack experience. When Browning was twenty-four years old, he published two poems which he called *Madhouse Cells*. One described a theologian who believed in predestination, the other described a lover who murdered the woman of his heart. Later in life, Browning reprinted these poems, but omitted the title. As he grew older and observed how many individualists walk the streets, he became more and more unwilling to call anyone insane. Wise men and women, as they descend into the vale of years, become more and more tolerant, that is, more and more sensible.

Just as a variety of human relations enables one to live more abundantly, so a continuance of alert interest in a variety of subjects enables one to live longer. I mean just exactly what I say. Physically all who have passed forty begin to deteriorate; there is no way to prevent it; although people differ very much in their comparative power of bodily activity. But mentally some men and women never grow old, no matter how many years they have to their credit. If they maintain a constant interest in the world about them they will actually live longer than those whose curiosity diminishes or decays.

I think I can point out the exact moment when a man begins to grow old. It is the moment, when, upon self-examination, he finds that his thoughts and reflexions in solitude turn more to the past than to the future. If a man's mind is more filled with memories and reminiscences than with anticipation, then he is growing old.

This need never be the case. A few weeks ago I called on a gentleman in Boston, who in a few months will be ninety. As I came into his library he was vigorously playing the typewriter. He rose, greeted me cordially, and we had a lively conversation about current affairs.

There are old men and women whose minds are fully as powerful as in the days of their youth; but their minds have lost alertness, resilience; if the conversation continues on a certain theme, they can hold up their end and do their part; but if the theme of talk changes rapidly from this to that, as it so often does, they are left behind. I believe that this loss of mental agility, in the majority of cases, need not happen. One must watch oneself, and not fall a victim either to the garrulity or the egotism of decrepitude. One should always remain a person and never become a personage. My Bostonian changed from one topic to another with the ease and springiness of youth.

Many years ago I was invited by my friend Mr. Richard B. Glaenzer to meet the great French actor Constant Coquelin, who was then playing in New York. It was a large dinner party, and though we all did homage to the guest of honour, there was another man present who aroused in my mind even greater wonder and enthusiasm. He was that magnificent American, John Bigelow, who forty years before, had been American Minister to France. He was now ninety years of age. Never shall I forget him as he appeared on that evening. Long after midnight he sat beside. Coquelin. He was smoking a huge black cigar and chattering French with the great actor, with all the vitality and sparkle of youth. John Bigelow never had time to grow old.. He was too constantly interested in an immense variety of contemporary ideas and things.

John Bigelow was an intellectual athlete; but a continuous and keen interest in life will prevent the advances of age in a bodily athlete. The former prize-fighter, James J. Corbett, is now well over sixty; he is more interesting to meet and talk with than when he was young. His auto biography, *The Roar o f the Crowd,* is a valuable contribution to psychology; for it shows that Corbett has always been as much interested in human nature as if he were a novelist or playwright. Some years ago, I was dining in the Hotel Grunewald in New Orleans, when I saw Mr. Corbett enter at the other end of the room. I said to my table-companion, "That's Jim Corbett!" and the waiter, thinking I had an appointment with him, brought him at once to my table. Well, I found him a more interesting man than the ordinary casual acquaintance; he was interesting because his mind was so quick and agile-what I call a prehensile mind.

The old-fashioned shoe-maker or cobbler was invariably an interesting man; I suppose that his labour being mechanical, he had plenty of time to *think,* which with many busy people has become a lost art. When I was a boy, I had only one pair of shoes at a time; so when these needed to be cobbled, I had to sit an hour or two hours with the shoemaker, while he soled and heeled my shoes. I always found him entertaining. He had meditated and reflected long and deeply, and I reaped the harvest of his solitary hours.

One of the most intelligent men I ever knew could neither

read nor write. He was a coast-guardsman in Michigan, a member of a life-saving crew, and his name was Sam Neal.

His long hours on duty at all hours of the day and night were filled with meditations on life and human nature. He had immense common sense, excellent practical judgement, and what he knew he knew thoroughly. He had pondered, sometimes sadly, more often humorously, on various types of men and on human experience. I learned much from him, and it was a delight to hear him talk.

Bernard Shaw, who hates and despises all forms of competitive athletic sports, like football, tennis, golf, etc., says that nearly all men are no better than playboys. That we never grow up. That even when we reach the age of seventy, we are still interested in childish things. This is of course true, but perhaps if we were not interested in sport, we should be no better for the lack of it. Still, to any student of human nature, the enormous place taken by sport in the life of the average man is food for reflexion. During the most exciting period of the World War, I was travelling on a train in Illinois. The morning came, and we were all eager to get the news. Finally a boy appeared, bringing the Chicago morning papers. Sitting next to me was a clergyman, in ecclesiastical uniform. He bought a paper, and without looking at the first page, turned excitedly to the sporting columns and read the chronicles of yesterday's games. Not only do millions of fairly civilised persons read the sporting pages every day, but men who are quite intelligent in other respects, are enormously elated by a victory in golf, and correspondingly depressed by defeat. This emotion is unreasonable. If we were reasonable creatures, we should not particularly care. We should say, '(Oh) it's only a game, and I have had the fresh air, good company, and pleasant recreation." But whoever saw a golf-player who talked or felt like that?

The late Professor William D. Whitney, the former Sanscrit scholar in the world, author of a long list of learned books, member of any number of learned European societies, was finally forbidden by his doctor to play any game, croquet, checkers, cards, or what not, because he suffered such agony when defeated that it had a disastrous effect on his nerves and mental energy.

A prominent banker in a midwestern city was an excellent businessman. He was serious, dignified, and wise. He had the respect of all who knew him; he was a pillar of society. Well, one day he was playing golf for a little recreation. He made a miserable shot with his brassy. He leaped up and down in a transport of rage, broke the club in two, and then bit it with savage fury.

Three friends of mine were playing golf with a famous nerve specialist. On their way through the green and pleasant land, the doctor told the other men that golf was a splendid thing if one did not take it too seriously. "It is a pity," said he, "that men cannot remember that, after all, it is only a game. If they play well, all right; if they play badly, let them not get excited. For if one takes golf too seriously, it does far more harm than good." Shortly after he had completed this homily, the players came to a tee where they had to drive across a lake. The doctor drove into the water. He laughed and drove another ball into the water. This time he did not laugh, but drove a third ball into the water. Then he cursed, threw every one of his clubs into the lake, threw the golf bag after them, and walked loudly away to the clubhouse. Such is life. Such indeed it really is.

There is no study more interesting than the study of human nature. But in order to have even a little knowledge and understanding of this illimitable theme, one must in imagination put oneself in the other man's place. I think one reason why so many people appear stupid or silly or crazy to onlookers is that the onlooker remains aloof-he does not share their experience. Unless one does in imagination get inside the other man's mind, one will remain in ignorance.

Many satirical novels and plays come from an aloof (and therefore ignorant) observation of human nature. Briefly, the novelist in this instance does not understand the game. For example: suppose you are watching two respectable middle-aged men playing chess. You have never seen a game of chess. You know nothing about it. You don't know the difference between a bishop and a pawn. Well, you see one man push a tiny wooden figure, and the other man exhibit signs of acute dismay. Suddenly a look of rapturous triumph comes

into his face, and he makes a move and the other man collapses. Of course you think both men are idiotic. Well, they are not; you do not understand the game.

You see and overhear two young lovers. Their conversation appears to be the last word in imbecility. That is because you are not in love. You laugh at them, but if you are in love yourself, you don't laugh; because love, whatever transport it may contain, has no humour. You watch a Salvation Army evangelist address a street crowd and become terribly excited. You look on from what you regard as a superior intellectual standpoint. But what this really means is that you haven't got his form of religion. In other words, you are ignorant. The realistic and satirical novelist describes an evangelist in bitter mockery, because the novelist has no religion, and therefore cannot share the other's fervour. But suppose this very evangelist could overhear the novelist discussing with some cronies in Greenwich Village "the art of the novel," and becoming terribly heated in the discussion, what would the evangelist think of such twaddle?

To a person who cares nothing about politics, a man in a state of political excitement appears silly. So one might go through the whole range of human passions, interests, and obsessions. What then is the answer? The answer is that if one really wishes to study human nature effectively, one must study it sympathetically. This is why Saint Paul said that Charity was greater than Faith or Hope. By Charity he meant intellectual sympathy, the capacity to enter without prejudice into another's state of mind.

Finally, in spite of the selfish instincts of human nature, in spite of the bad record of every nation in the past and in the present, in spite of swindlers, liars, cowards, thieves, and murderers, it is with a thrill of admiration that we recall the names of certain individuals who have in their own lives and characters revealed the heroic possibilities of human nature; all men and women are potentially sublime, for every one has the divine spark.

www.ingramcontent.com/pod-product-compliance
Lightning Source LLC
La Vergne TN
LVHW041239080426
835508LV00011B/1286